I Love Sports

Surfing

by Erika S. Manley

Bullfrog Books

Ideas for Parents and Teachers

Bullfrog Books let children practice reading informational text at the earliest reading levels. Repetition, familiar words, and photo labels support early readers.

Before Reading

- Discuss the cover photo. What does it tell them?

- Look at the picture glossary together. Read and discuss the words.

Read the Book

- "Walk" through the book and look at the photos. Let the child ask questions. Point out the photo labels.

- Read the book to the child, or have him or her read independently.

After Reading

- Prompt the child to think more. Ask: Have you ever seen surfers in action? Have you wanted to try?

Bullfrog Books are published by Jump!
5357 Penn Avenue South
Minneapolis, MN 55419
www.jumplibrary.com

Library of Congress Cataloging-in-Publication Data

Names: Manley, Erika S., author.
Title: Surfing / by Erika S. Manley.
Description: Bullfrog Books Edition. Minneapolis, Minnesota : Jump!, Inc., [2018] | Series: I Love Sports | Includes index. | Audience: Ages: 5–8. Audience: Grades: K to Grade 3. | Identifiers: LCCN 2017032110 (print) | LCCN 2017028595 (ebook) | ISBN 9781624966712 (ebook) ISBN 9781620318232 (hardcover : alk. paper) | Subjects: LCSH: Surfing—Juvenile literature. Surfing—Miscellanea—Juvenile literature. Classification: LCC GV840.S8 (print) LCC GV840.S8 M26 2018 (ebook) | DDC 797.3/2—dc23 LC record available at https://lccn.loc.gov/2017032110

Editor: Jenna Trnka
Book Designer: Leah Sanders
Photo Researcher: Leah Sanders

Photo Credits: Comstock Images/Getty, cover; smashgold/Shutterstock, 1; TAGSTOCK1/iStock, 3; EpicStockMedia/iStock, 4; Paul Topp/Dreamstime, 5; J_K/Shutterstock, 6–7, 16–17, 23tl, 23br; AkilinaWinner/iStock, 7, 23tr; Alena Ozerova/Dreamstime, 8, 9, 23bl; Sollina Images/Getty, 10–11, 12–13; WoodysPhotos/Shutterstock, 14–15; Paul Nicklen/Getty, 18, 19; Henrique NDR Martins/iStock, 20–21; Ferli Achirulli/123rf, 22; wavebreakmedia/Shutterstock, 24.

Printed in the United States of America at Corporate Graphics in North Mankato, Minnesota.

Table of Contents

Let's Surf!

Grab your board.

Let's go to the beach!

Let's surf!

leash ·····▶

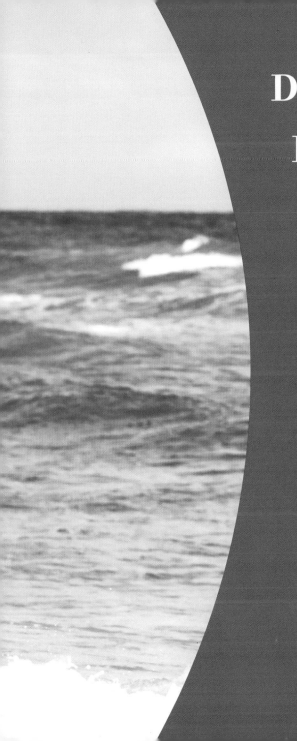

Dan waxes his board.

It keeps his feet
from slipping.

He wears a leash.

It connects to
the board.

All set!

wax

Mia paddles out.

She turns
her board.

It faces shore.

She waits.

Here comes a wave!
Luke lies down.
He paddles.
Go fast!

Time to pop up!

Luke jumps up.

He bends
his knees.

North Palm Beach L

He spreads his feet.

He leans forward.

Wipeout!
That is OK.

Tam waits
for a wave.

18

Here is one!

Tam rides it.

Surfing is fun!

Do you want to try?

Surfing Equipment

wetsuit

surfboard

leash

Picture Glossary

leash
A rope that attaches a surfer to his or her board.

waxes
Rubs wax on a surfboard to keep the surface less slippery.

paddles
Uses one's arms to propel the surfboard in the water.

wipeout
Falling off or being knocked off a surfboard.

Index

To Learn More

Learning more is as easy as 1, 2, 3.

1) Go to www.factsurfer.com

2) Enter "surfing" into the search box.

3) Click the "Surf" button to see a list of websites.

With factsurfer.com, finding more information is just a click away.